Faith and Family

Merci Van Raden

 BookLeaf Publishing

Presentation by *BookLeaf Publishing*

Web: www.bookleafpub.com

E-mail: info@bookleafpub.com

ISBN: 9789357610834

First edition 2022

DEDICATION

Aunt Bee, I miss you every single day. Thank you for being the best pen pal ever for ten years. Happy Trails!

The True Meaning of Love

My Nana and Papa were married for fifty-one
years,
Through this time they both shed a few tears.
Ron and Jane were married on May 15,
Nana's dress was a sight to be seen.
Melissa was there first girl,
She always loved to chase a squirrel.
Marcy was their second child.
Sometimes she was gentle, other times she was
wild.
Tommy was there first and last boy,
Oh, but raising him was their pride and joy.
When Tommy was four,
He wanted to know more,
About how Jesus dies on the cross for our sin
and is now alive for ever more.
It was such a wonderful day,
When Tommy got saved.
At four and a half Tommy died.
Nana sat in disbelief and cried.
Little did Nana know God was giving her a test,
To prove to her that HIS way is ALWAYS best!
Nana chose right,
And searched the Scriptures for answers both
day and night.
Papa chose wrong,

And started smoking and drinking all day long.
Nana took Melissa and Marcy,
To church whenever it was open you see.
Pastor Spencer and his wife,
Visited Nana to teach her how to grow in her
spiritual life.
When Pastor Spencer talked to Papa in the shed,
Papa wouldn't really listen or nod his head.
Years later when the kids were all married and
grown,
Nana showed a love to Papa, just like Christ had
shown.
When Papa got cancer,
He wouldn't even answer.
Just before he died,
Nana once more tried.
"Ron, are you going to accept Jesus Christ as
your Savior?"
When Papa told her he did,
All of Nana's burden and tears slid
My Nana chose the better part,
For she taught me the true meaning of a
servant's heart.

Joy Through Adversity

In the world there is a lot of sickness, death, and
pain,
But, through this all, one thing remains the
same.
Jesus Christ, God's only Son,
Loves us each and every one!
When we ask Jesus to come into our heart,
This is when true joy will start.
We read in the Bible about Paul,
Who didn't let adversity hinder him at all.
Even when on every side of him was a prison
wall.
Paul wrote many books of the Bible that are an
encouragement to us all,
No matter how big or small.
There are many reasons to have joy today,
Some are being able to read our Bible and pray.
Another example is Jesus our Savior and King,
He also served God through everything.
When our day seems hopeless or sad,
We can trust God to make us glad.
No matter what we go through,
God will always be there for you.
If we read our Bible and pray,
God will give us strength throughout the day.

If you feel down in your gloom,
Remember Jesus rose again-there is an empty
tomb.
And always remember to smile,
It doesn't hurt every once in awhile.

Trusting God

It is easy to trust God if my day is good,
Or if I do the things I should.
Things like reading my Bible every day,
And always making sure to pray.
If everything goes wrong,
I walk around and my face looks long.
During these times I need to trust God for a
song.
And He will give me one all the day long.
I have lots to be thankful for from above,
Including God's omnipotent love.
I'm not Paul or Silas in jail,
Nor am I weak or frail.
God help me through the week,
To always in your Word seek.

Look to God

When it feels like your world is falling apart,
And you don't know where to start.
Look to God!
He's the one who understands our deepest pain.
Without Him our life would not be the same.
When we need to cry,
God will hear!
For He is always near.
God knows what we need before we ask,
He will help us until the hard time is past.
So next time you are feeling low,
And you feel like you have no friends here below,
Look to God!

God's Way is Best

When there are things in life we don't
understand,
We must always remember God has a plan.
God promises to hear us when we pray,
And He will listen to us every single day.
Jesus listens and sees when we cry,
He even hears the smallest sigh.
Troubles will come and troubles will go,
But, through it all God's love will show.
Whether it be sickness, death, or pain,
God will remain the same!
Next time something doesn't go as planned,
Take it to God; He will understand!

That's My God

Who created the earth in just six days?
Who can calm the crashing waves?
Who made the blind to see?
Who sent Jesus to save you and me?
He is the beginning and the end,
But, He's also my best friend.
That's My God!
Who made all the birds to sing.
That's My God!
He's the King of Kings!
Let everyone tell His praises wherever they go,
That others might know,
That's My God!
Who turned the water into wine?
Who's face began to shine?
The one who invites all to "come and dine."
The man who laid down His life for you and
mine.
May I spread His love through the world,
No matter how many cruel words are hurled.
My God is greater than it all,
And with His help I will stand tall.
Whether it be passing out a tract or speaking of
His glorious name,
May I never of Him be ashamed.

Best Friends

There are important people you always need in
your life,
And I don't necessarily need your husband or
wife.
Those people I am talking about are your best
friends,
People you can talk or laugh with hours on end.
Whether they lend you their shoulder so you can
cry,
Or if they give you all their fries.
Best friends make you feel better fast,
So sad times don't ever last.
They are the first people willing to take an
impromptu shopping trip,
But, also the people to laugh first when you slip.
Blasting music with the windows down,
So the music can be heard all through the town.
The talks late into the night,
Best friends make everything right.

Blackie

Many things can be called a man's best friend,
It can be a person or an animal-it just depends.
But, for my dad it was his 1997 ford ranger.,
To him this truck was no stranger.
Dad listened fondly to every sound the truck
would make.
He understood it-even when it would shake.
We named the truck "Blackie" for obvious
reasons.
All of us kids fought to ride with Dad no matter
the reason.
From carrying spices, mulch, and cans.
Blackie worked harder for my dad than he did
for any other man.
When Charity left for college in 2012,
Blackie took a trip he later learned so well.
When Blackie split down the middle,
Dad fixed him with not so much a giggle.
When the transmission went out it made us all
sad,
As for people who cried-just my Dad.
Blackie ended up with 406, 419 miles,
Nobody is going to beat that record for a long
while.
Well Blackie you will be missed,

I really wish I could've given you a goodbye kiss.

Fall

Here comes a nice, gentle breeze,
Sweeping all the leaves from off the trees.
As the leaves float through the air,
Some land of people's hair.
Others land on people as they talk,
Whether it be in their yard or sidewalk.
Down the road a parent rakes another leaf pile,
Just for it to be jumped in by a child.
Crinkle and crunch,
Another baby has tried to eat a leaf although
they had lunch.
Pumpkin pie, pumpkin cake,
And all the other fall desserts you can bake.
Marshmallows being made into smores over the
fire,
Girls posting pictures of their smores on their
Instagram for others to admire.
Fall is just like the earth's great big hug,
And all the flannels and jackets make one feel as
warm as a bug.

Covid 19

Everyone's life seemed normal and good,
And everything seemed to be going the way it
should.
Then all of a sudden out of the blue,
Covid 19 came to me and you.
People were now stuck in their home,
And all they could do was groan.
Where did all the t.p. go,
It is a covid 19 thing you know.
Unable to see family and friends,
When will covid 19 end?
Unpredictable happenings, crazy days,
I just hope covid will soon go away.

A Different Look at Horses

Watch the horses as they neigh,
Do you ever wonder what they say.
Sometimes they talk while eating their hay,
I wonder if the older ones say,
"What did you say?"
When kids feed them grass,
Many of the horses pass gas.
And with this coronoa..do the horses have to wear a mask?
I guess it won't hurt to ask

Small Towns

In small towns everyone is your friend,
They stop you in the street and ask you how
your day has been.
Everyone wants to be there for you,
No matter what you do.
People who start a conservation with you in the
store,
And pull together to help the poor.
Small town people are sweet and kind,
Friends like them are hard to find.

The Water Issue

A certain guest at the hotel,
Didn't start off to well.
The water was supposed to be hot,
But it absolutely was not.
Moving guests from room to room,
Just created more gloom.
A certain guest finally moved to first floor,
He didn't want to move anymore.
The next day was a better day,
The hot water began working-hooray!
No matter what problem come and go,
Guests will always know,
Quality Inn and Suites is the place to be,
For all one's needs.

The Walk

17

While walking there is much one can see or
hear,
Depending on what time one walks one might
see some deer.
The smell of fresh cut grass is such a great
smell,
But, I love the smell of laundry as well!
Children are out riding their bikes,
Or some are playing baseball-don't get a strike.
Hearing the train as it rumbles on past,
Mothers soaking up the sun and letting every
second last.

Smiles

Did you ever see someone who looked sad?
Or as if their day had gone bad?
The way to help is easy-
All you have to is smile,
It won't even take you a long while.
A smile can help them have a better day,
As they go on their way.
So smile!
Don't be full of fear,
Bring some cheer!
So next time you seem someone who looks sad,
Try to make them become glad!

Gene

I was just a neighbor, for many years,
Until I walked over with fear.
I carried over the banana-nut bread,
Just like my mom said.
When I gave it to Gene,
Little did I know what it would come to mean.
Week after week, I made the bread,
I always heard Karen as she said,
"Gene, your sweetie is here."
Little did I know, how much I would miss,
Those words and Gene's hug.
Though when I hugged him, I felt squashed-
Just like a bug.
Of course, when Gene hugged me, Karen
wanted one to,
I loved them both so that was easy to do.
When I saw an ambulance, Labor Day 2016,
I was afraid of what it would mean.
When I heard Gene died, I just cried,
Why make banana bread again, I sighed.
But, God said to me, "Karen is still alive."
For me, it will be hard to make banana bread
again,
But to Karen it means a million,
So, I will never end.

Now Karen will get all the hugs,
If Darla doesn't interfere.

Michael D. Ryan aka Cookie Monster

Green pants, a black jacket, and a hat.
Who would I be describing with that?
        Why! Mike Ryan a kind man.
Who I'm going to miss more than you can
understand.
        When my Dad told me that Mike had
died,
I just sat there and cried.
        Mike didn't have many friends no,
But, the few he had– he let his love for them
show.
        By princess waving in a parade,
To giving me a hug on Saturday.
        He loved his country the USA,
Mike was a proud Navy SEAL to his last day.
        He was drafted into the military in 1969.
He worked for the Navy SEALs for a long time.
        Mike was in active duty during
Operation Desert Storm/Desert Shield.
And to the enemy he would never yield.
        Mike didn't officially retire until 2010,
We could talk about his great service for our
country hours on end.

I used to make Mike cookies-I don't remember what kind,-
But, he would give me hugs and of course I wouldn't mind.
Yes, I lost a great friend,
But, I hope that I will be able to see him again.

Garrett Rocky Hicks

Garrett Rocky Hicks" "Mercy nooo"

Oh how all these memories are starting to show.

From nerf wars during ladies Bible study,

To riding in Alex's jeep getting muddy.

Drawing during Sunday school,

We never got caught so that's cool.

Being mistaken as your twin,

Anytime when we would soul win.

When you were the bus captain your circle of
influence grew,

Girls on the bus falling in love you.

 Alex, Connor, and I saying "ew."

Having a ugly toes contest on the bus,

And everything time it was boiled down to just us.

Working at the inn was always fun,

Even tho we would talk more then getting the work done.

Having you clean bathrooms at the inn,

You and I seeing who can carry up the most Christmas bins.

(Mr. OCD) Having dishes just so

Always eating chicken Alfredo.

Going on the college trip was fun,

Especially seeing Brother Mund.

That's where we talked about being Lego women and men,

And when you and Connor had push up contests until Pastor put that to an end.

You also had grits for the first time,

You stole all of mine.

When I was in college 2018-2020,

I missed you so much it wasn't even funny.

But in 2020, you texted me some great news.

No, it wasn't that you got new shoes.

You were dating the love of your life,

And were excited that she was going to be your wife.

On August 27, of 2021,

These two wonderful people became one.

Oh Garrett with your quick smile and easy laugh,

I have many memories I can think of just like that.

I can't wait to see you again in Heaven some day,

But until then, I'll miss you every day.